Speaking in Midnight Tongues

and Other Symptoms of Neon Fever

poetry & essays by

Miles Mendoza

Speaking in Midnight Tongues
and Other Symptoms of Neon Fever
Copyright © 2021 by Miles Louis Mendoza

This is a work of fiction. Names, characters, places, and incidents either are the product of the author's imagination or are used fictitiously. Any resemblance to actual persons, living or dead, events, or locales is entirely coincidental.

First paperback edition September 2021
from Mendoza Press

*Illustrations, Book Cover, and Title Design
by Pedro Gomes*

ISBN 978-1-7379149-0-7 (paperback)
ISBN 978-1-7379149-1-4 (ebook)

For my grandmother, Maria,
who led me by the hand into a world of words

Speaking in Midnight Tongues

and
Other
Symptoms
of Neon Fever

Contents

The author of this book of poetry knows it is just one amongst many books of poetry. The author of this book of poetry is fully aware that in the process of finding your way to this very description, you're liable to have tripped over a pile of love ballads, wannabe Bukowskis, and other creative hopefuls maligning the state of the world. The author of this book of poetry imagines you've read along as the many before him bemoaned their vices, romantic failures, and resulting insecurities. The author of this book of poetry also expects you might have already read a thing or two about addiction, war, and modern masculinity.

However, while the author of this book of poetry does in fact write about the above topics (as well as gentrification, racial identity, and the search for beauty in a city he does not always understand but is determined to love), it is important to him that you know he attempted to do so while veins of undiluted faith in you, the reader, pumped right into his neon heart.

The author of this book of poetry trusts you're here for something new. The author of this book of poetry wants to blur what you have come to know as poetry with the world of the occult, the eldritch, the strange, the cosmic, the senseless, and the lawless. The author of this book of poetry thinks you're ready for dead gods, avatar canines, blind dates with linguivores, and talking rats in the desert. The author of this book of poetry wants to get straight up weird with you.

The author of this book of poetry is absolutely terrified by the idea of having written just another book of poetry. The author of this book of poetry is all too aware of the hubris baked into any attempts to do otherwise yet the author of this book of poetry was, apparently, not so easily dissuaded. It should be known, the author of this book of poetry is regularly and effortlessly seduced by such highly motivating factors as the deep-seated fear of irrelevance, barely constrained egomania, and a need for a little bit of cash.

The author of this book of poetry offers you a book of poetry unlike any you've read before. Or maybe it's just like all the rest and by the time you figure that out- it will be too late.

So, what do you think?

Do you, dear reader, have the same confidence in the author of this book of poetry as he had in you while writing it?

Let's find out.

Call of The Bard

Not for the first time,
the bentward designs
of my mind beckon for me
to shave the ready-raw skin of my teeth
as if my every thought
were a hotwire job gone wrong,
as if mine Caesar's Reign of
this body hath come full senate circle,
as if the seance lull
of The Three-Sisters Promise
could produce for me kingdom eternal
if I could but rid myself of these tired bones.

Exotic Fruit

For the first time in a long time, I have a loaded weapon slung across my chest. The air is humid but not in a smothering way. It begs me to remember the Carolinas where I trained for years with more affinity than they deserve.

What are you? Who are you? Where are you from?
Why are you here.
You ask the other man stuck on a shit detail with you things like this.
It is how we say to one another "I see you. I accept you for this trusted position in this trying time."
Why are we here.

"I'm Mexican." We are both _Mexican_.
We are apparently two _Mexican_ men in American uniforms protecting Puerto Rican land from Puerto Rican intruders.

"They come in on horseback," we were told.
"Over the mountains. They want the brass from the ammo. Shoot a warning shot first."

Puerto Rican cowboys gather on the fringes of my imagination as they discuss the ironies of the brown men standing between them and their pennies.

Telepathically, I tell them

"I won't shoot. I don't hate you for being poor. I won't shoot. Also… I am afraid of hitting the horse."

If I close my eyes, I can hear the waves of the ocean. It's the same ocean that rolls in on the coast of the Rockaways. The same waves. Yet, here they are exotic. And everyone knows exotic is another word for magic.

So, I listen to the magic waves that are much too far away for me to hear and I warn my telepathic cowboy friends in the dark.

Nothing in this world can be right. And yet I have found happiness.
This world is wrong. But it has carved out within itself room for me to be wrong with it.
Who am I to complain?
Who am I?

Before leaving us to our sentry state of mind, the same officer who described to us brown skinned men the Puerto Rican plight (and the horseman form it has chosen) walked over to a tree in the distance.

In the twilight, I watched him pluck from it a mango.
"It isn't ripe!" he called back.

He took it with him anyway.

My Relic Renaissance

A crescent moon hangs
low and ancient
in its manifestation but
that has jack-shit
to do with fuck-all
because the only relic
shining white-hot tonight
is your own face,
wet with glitch code
programmed for the lust of
all the things we're now
supposed to hate:
It's been too many nights since
The last threat bloodied;
The last hunt wildered;
The last damsel distressed.

Every second of peace is an eon
when the tachycardic rhythm
you trained into your heart is that
of the Sinister Spindrift Syndicate
and other such outdated
shogun sympathies.

Leech

I was reborn
in your Bethlehem
and swung from the
heights of mine Gotham
but long has it been
since a dusk has past
whence upon I had
the dark delight of counting
myself lost amongst
these spires and shrines
to the angry charm of a new empire dream.

I promised myself,
passing the bridge
between
your heart and belly,
if I ever sullied myself
with the sin of suspicion
that I might have
discovered every decorative inch
you had attempted
to keep from me,
consumed every secret
you would hoard away
from my hungry lips, I would

extinguish the flames of hubris
dancing upon my skin
with the waters of abandonment.

Tell me there is yet more
to bleed from you,
so this parasite might remain.

Lie to me.

Of Vice and Verve

There is a moment
when your breath
crackles, hums with
synth and you know,
you know you know
what's coming next
even if you've never
known exactly where from.

You've suffered and
exalted in the neon mirth
of many a-a-addiction,
retreats into delusions most grand
but nothing conjures a
cacophony in the neural network
quite like
the chopped up white electric
line of a new idea.

Eyes illuminant and
nerves drowning in powdered
reverb, the world
synchronized with your ego
-divinity flowing in place
of blood and doubt-

generating that moment,
just one fleeting moment
when you no longer aspire.

You simply are what
you were meant to be:
Creation given form,
God in the body of a lie.

Fuck Orpheus

I am an electric riff on a pawned guitar, dripping in style and
humming of failure.
I am a rehashed verse, a chorus stolen- a lazy refrain filthier
than the needle in the arm of my corner crazy.
I am a song as old as man, a tune carried by bards drafted
into battle,
seduced by the promise of spiced wine.
I am nothing new.
I am the guy that would rather die
than be found derivative.
I am the scion of the unkillable syllable:
The second coming of the
never got going.
I'm a poet. We write, fight, and lie.
I'm a poet. What horrible luck.
I'm a poet.

Heat Death and Other Clues

I must need some sleep.
Or perhaps,

I'm watching my sanity unfurl
in the shape of the daisy-dragon's
hot breath as I find myself enlisted
yet again in hologram missions like some
detective for the paradox agency,
a cosmic mystery's cool blue hands
around my neck smelling of
living smoke: concocting a
Chaos conspiracy theory the shape of
Death wearing an electric trench coat.

Or perhaps,
I just need some sleep.

The Shine

I write from a place of desperation.
I spend time up against walls.
A gun to my head daring
myself to "prove it."
So I grab some memory,
some trauma, some guilt
by the collar and I drag it out back
to bury it alive under loose words.

The real bastards die hard, keep right
on pulling at the heartstrings
as you smooth out the punctuation-
But nothing, not a damn thing
survives the weight of the edit.
That takes the shine right out.

Oh god, and let me read it aloud.
It's like it never happened at all.
They call this closure.
But really it's a dirty
deal with a derelict devil,
the lord of the shameless
demanding the same damned act
writers have always been willing
to make of the world around them:

Sacrifice.

The End of Slumber

These Saturday nights are for
grind-heart salutations to
forgotten gods and translating
inverted scripts plied from
lost continents.

These Sāturni diēs moons are for
Eastern mysteries in southbound
hands, dark algebra scribbled
on kidnapped destinies.

These Sunnanæfen hours are for
the long wrath of kings strangled
in cribs finding resurrection
in the madness of lowmen-mages
deep in their cups.

Cronus wakes.
Gather yourselves for The Games.

Supper

Her lips smack of good diction and her teeth shine with the grease of well seasoned syllables. As she takes the seat across the table, my words flee from my mind as if sensing an approaching predator.

I order a drink to entice them back while she interrogates the Maitre D' about the house's selection of prose. Her chest heaves with anticipation as he lists the night's special: southern-gothic with an early Marquez marinade.

What I at first believed to be tattoos reveal themselves to be flavorful morsels, tucked away for future snacking, as she errantly plucks them from her skin and swallows them whole. She eyes me like I might be hiding future additions to her collection in my pockets. The ink on my own skin begins to crawl beneath my shirt, signaling nescient plans of retreat.

"Well, say something, you fool," she whispers across the table. The line of dialogue slips out her mouth, deluded with dreams of escape. She pays me little mind while grabbing it effortlessly by the tail. My stomach turns as I watch her break its spine at the comma, leaving it convulsing on the tablecloth between us.

As she digs her knife into a tender vowel, I realize she's beautiful in the way only lethal things are capable: like an antique pistol some eccentric author might keep on his mantle should the need for a murder-suicide present itself.

"What happened? I heard you were quite the smooth talker," she says with a mouthful of her own taunts. A belch produces a mist of Burroughs from her throat and I know then I will die this night.

My brow begins to sweat as any attempt I make at replying is quashed by a resurgent childhood stutter, an instinctual form of self-preservation. Relinquishing myself to the inevitable, I wonder which stage of grief involves awe of your destroyer.

I stare at my empty plate as I listen to her suck the marrow out of her own words before letting them drip from her mouth. "Oh honey, don't worry." I gather my courage and look up to see her picking her teeth with stray punctuation. She slides me a tray of "I know how to pry what I want out of you," as if daring me to make a break for the door.

I know I'll never make it. I have always been known as a man of many words and it is clear now The Woman Who Eats Language Alive has long caught my scent.

Particular

I found her poetry last night
though, I wish I hadn't

These tributes of passion,
secretly scrawled and
kept so well hidden away,
made me all too aware
of how capable her
heart is of love
and just how little of it
I have inspired in her

I saw what it looks like when
her soul puts on
that particular dress and
just how naked
and ashamed
she must feel before me

Murder Me

You said you hated Christmas.

Of all things: Christmas!
You had taken me out
that night, after you realized
the reason I was always
broke was the payments
on that damn car in California.
The one for my parents.
The one that would eventually get towed.

You thought it was sweet.
You thought I was sweet.
Just not sweet enough
to make up for a lack
of degree, fortune, faith
and blue eyes.
Just not sweet enough to meet your mom.

We were tequila soaked.
And you said you hated
the way people celebrated Christmas.
Wasn't Christ-like enough.
Which was funny to me.
I asked why Christ never

seemed to come up
in my Bushwick bed
or the back of that taxi on my birthday.

That's when I realized
I was just a secret, one
you were going to have
to murder in a confessional some day.

Now I hate Christmas, too.

The Dim-Beat Call

This vassal of creativity
has never known
the kiss of a lyrical education
but there is a
melody born of manic entropy
strumming its anarchist rhythm
through my veins tonight
and if these lips were to part
I fear the warsong knell rung
will beg the appetite of
ancient desires driven by
blackfire enginehearts
no hitherto known
age of enlightenment
could hold a candle to.

Micro

I dip my cup into the
Stream of Consciousness
and Lazy Metaphors
and find it full instead
with analogies and other microplastics
because nothing
has mattered since that dude
(who somehow manages to
simultaneously quote himself
and plagiarize others all at once)
got a publishing deal.

I suppose me and my
Cronenberg-body of work
can take our
clever cosmological concoctions
and go fuck ourselves,
so long as we're all on the same page
because remember:
consent is sexy.

My cup runneth over
   runneth over
   runneth over.
     But, as a people,

we're now past
the point of thirst.

I hate you all.

No Heroes Here

"I can't get away from this nigger!"
He was referring to the President as he gave the State of the Union Address.

Those words have circled me like a school of taunting predators for the better part of a decade. They rest, patient, atop a sea of silence. They will go nowhere, having caught the scent of complicity in the water.

This isn't a war story.
We were in Afghanistan, draped in digicam, weapons on our hip.
But this isn't a war story.

Corporal Linden, who spoke those words, is dead now. Belly full of a 30 rack, he shot himself in the head to prove to his girlfriend he had it in him to do it. At least, that's what I was told when I got the call while shopping at Target. Sounded true to style. I never questioned it. Just hung up the phone and continued to browse.

This isn't a war story.
Death. Hate and cowardice. Just another slice of Americana in Eurasia.
But this isn't a war story.

I hate that I'm giving him a pseudonym. Corporal whatever the fuck Linden.

I truly don't remember his first name.

No one in this story deserves anonymity, least of all myself.

And yet…

Jesus. I don't even remember his first name.

I don't ever remember seeing him at the gym. But he was a strong guy.

Had a voice that could shake the roof off a house.

185 pounds of rage.

From Maine, lived and breathed hard work. We couldn't be more different.

Loved cheap beer, hated the corps. Okay, we had that in common.

Corporal Young worshipped the ground Linden walked on. Maybe that's why he's dead, too.

I don't know the story there. But I called Young's phone number on accident once.

His dad answered. I told him I dialed the wrong number. He said "No, you haven't, son."

Called me son. Asked if I needed anything. Said the boy never got over losing "Richy."

Called me son.

I went to the closest bar. Loved some cheap beer. Hated the Corps.
Barely made it home.
Called me son.

There were two groups of us. The techs and the mechs.
We spent all our time in an armory. I called it the batcave.
It had kangaroo rats. The mechs made a scoreboard to see who could kill the most.
I'd tell them to hide. They were there before we got there.
They would be there long after we left.
I called it the batcave. No heroes here.

Linden and I had a screaming match once. I went to the gym every day but I was still sure that a right hook from him could kill me. Not to mention the guns on our hip. So, there he was, shaking the roof. I can't remember what it was about. I wish it had been about the slur. I could tell you all about my moral fortitude. But I think it was just hot. So, I'm just another sweaty coward.

It took all the air in my lungs to outmatch his screams. "DO YOU THINK THE LOUDEST PERSON WINS?" I yelled, pounding my fist on the wooden bar between us, kicking the shelves. "HOW AM I DOING?"

He shut his mouth. My hands shook. He walked away.
We both knew something was coming.

Corporal Reynolds had watched the whole thing.

"You know those motherfuckers keep asking me what it was like to grow up poor?"

He was black. "Man, I'm telling you I grew up with two of everything."

He was black. "Bunch of racist motherfuckers."

He was black.

It's been seven years.

Reynolds still checks in on me.

He wasn't there when Linden called Obama a nigger.

He wasn't there when I said nothing.

Reynolds still checks in on me.

I don't answer anymore.

Some Marsoc Marines stopped by the armory that day. Marine Corps special forces. Pretty boys with prettier guns. They had some green beam dazzlers that needed servicing. High powered lasers that looked like lightsabers. Could burn a hole in the side of a tent if you let it sit there long enough. I inspected them while the sergeant told me how they would shine them in the eyes of children hundreds of yards away. They would wake up the next morning blind.

"Sorry, these need to be shipped back. Need modifications."

There wasn't anything wrong with his dazzlers. Blind-baby battle-ready.

"Aw, man. You sure? You don't have any to replace them with?"

I thought about the locker full of dazzlers in my office. "No. Fresh out."

I stayed in the armory that night. Didn't want to risk a confrontation with the mechs. I left the emergency-power red light on. Its soft, haunting glow was easier for your eyes to adjust to if you had to wake up fast. Shoot someone who'd climbed over the fence fast. I hated that red light. Made it hard to tell if you were dreaming or awake. I stared at the sticker displaying the Inspector General's tip line and wished I had it in me to dial it fast. Or at least dream I did.

I took out all the dazzlers. Broke every single one of them.

A kangaroo rat wandered into the office. I told it to hide. No heroes in this batcave.

The mechs showed up to the shop the next morning and selected an ambassador to approach me. "Hey. We're going on a run when we get back to the huts today. Want to come?"

A challenge. I accepted.

That evening, Reynolds asked me to change my mind.

"Don't go. They're going to jump you or something. Do you want me to come with you?"

I didn't. Couldn't risk it. I think I already knew what they wanted.
"Stay here. If I don't come back in a couple of hours…
I don't know. Just stay here."

They knocked on the door and I opened it. No one said anything. We stepped out into the sand and we started running. Linden took the lead. The sun set and took none of the heat with it. In the dark of the night, all you could hear was the beat of our feet as we headed to the perimeter of the base. No one dared breathe a heavy breath. No weakness. In the Marine Corps, if you can't run, you're nothing.
They thought I was nothing. They were there to show me I was nothing.
I let them have the first mile. I took the lead on the second. The third. Then the fourth.
I rounded the route back to the huts. Every one of them was ready to empty their lungs.
"Good run," Linden coughed.
"Yeah, good run. I'm going to keep going."
I ran back into the dark. Like a rat back into its hole.

This isn't a war story.

I had just taken my ACT's in a war zone. I was months away from being accepted to an ivy league college. A couple of years from dropping out of it. A very kind Sergeant I had spent the last 18 months living and training with was explaining to me that he would never allow my hypothetical son to date his very real daughter. Reynold's nonexistent children were also out of the question.

"Just wouldn't sit well with me," he explained to us.
I laughed. We laughed. We were all friends who laughed together.
They thought we were nothing and we believed them.
Reynolds still checks in on me.
I don't answer anymore.
I don't have any war stories.

Yoke

A flurry of fate had me disoriented
and I couldn't remember the last time
I tasted home but the sand
in my mouth told me I was
finally on native soil again as:
The only time I feel right
The only time I can get right
The only time I'm worth a damn
is when I'm playing renegade in the muck.

No, I didn't mind the yoke
or the warden who put it there.
It kept him as close to me as me to him.
All the while, as the bastard watched…

I composed his dread sonnet.

American Rot

For a lack of a crossroads,
I sold my soul in a strip mall
to a man with a uniform and
an impending arrest for statutory rape.

USA. USA. USA.

For a lack of ethos,
I bought into the mass hysteria
of Tarantino ultra-violence and
a troubling trend of designer drugs.

_(andthenthatguyatethe
otherguy'sfacedowninFlorida
andamarinenamedMittenswent
intoacomasoweallflushedourshit
andgotintosteroidsinstead)_

For a lack of fun,
we settled for hateful games
and digging holes in deserts
with no patience for our doxycycline dreams.

USA. USA. USA.

For a lack of
really anything at all
we raked youth and
pruned prejudice only
to feign surprise when that
garden bore so
little fruit.

Body of Debt

My nerves splinter:
static storms within the confines of my skull,
Macbeth's scorpions have come home to nest.
A growing temper begs my snarl as
this body has deemed services rendered,
thus payment owed.
This body has taken all forms.
This body has been beautiful and bloated.
This body has been lean and immortal.
This body has been bloody and beaten and alive with agony.
Yet, today I am less than an echo- a puddle of pity.
I was War! I was Rage! I was Glory!
My brown body weathered maelstroms for sport.
Now, it is a fallen oak whispering to passersby
of its roots, desperately clinging to the ecstasy
of the fray hidden in the memories of hurricanes past.

The Tug

Like a wartime lullaby
your coo rises within me
less a sense of security
than the solemn knowledge
a presence now lies in wait
just beyond the border
and I am left alone with
an urge most dreadful,
extending its fetid tendrils
throughout my body
and weary soul,
leaving in its wake
the blackprint outline
of a machine powered
by Dark Limerence,
its only purpose in being:

The assurance
that those at its
helm and mercy
will resist even
the most tempting
of Serenities.

Duhkha. Duhkha. Duhkha.

Trust Fun(d) Baby

I just want to write the easy shit
cigarette smoke in the air,
beer suds breaking under
our coke stuffed noses-
the things we already love.

I just want to write the fun shit, baby
sex on drugs, broken bras and
holes in the wall-
Quick! Honey, do that thing you do
where you overdose on medication
to get my attention.

O'god I want to write the good shit
before we kill your parents
and run off to Cabo
or somewhere else that
probably doesn't exist.

Speaking in Midnight Tongues

I can feel the witches on their gentrified rooftops with
their wine glasses in hand and PTA meetings wrapped up,
asking dead deities to align the planets while I'm just down
here willing to sign my firstborn over for a few good
signal lights, snapping my teeth at the scent of
adrenaline on the first warm night of a zombie winter
when I remember the man we called Big Ed or Big John
or Big Something and how he was larger than a house but
sweeter than a canned peach on a childhood
summer evening
carrying its twilight past axial possibility just the same as
I'm taking the curved corner of this street
faster than I should,
hoping there's dragon eyes waiting for me
around the bend even
as I remember Big Something holding his hands out like
his Sifu taught him,
asking me if I can see the energy between them and
his look of hurt
when I told him I couldn't see a thing but my mouth's
open now and
I'm coughing up third, fourth, and fifth eyes
because tonight's got
the taste of danger and even though the tank is running
low on pagan vocabulary,

I've got a carton of stolen white salamander synonyms
bouncing around the trunk,
so I wish you could see me now Big Something
because I've got enough
dusk in my pocket for the both of us to get right on
if I could just remember your goddamn name or
your goddamn anything
or if you were me or if I was you or if either of us
ever existed to begin with.

Centauri Proxima

Breathe.
How can you fight if you cannot…
Breathe.
How can you write if you cannot…
Breathe.
How can you exist if you cannot...

know walking this path
is like wandering past the proximity
of a small star radiating waves
of gravity and fire, full of
momentary singularities
begging as they beckon
to their bellies full of storm, yet another
Bright Baptism promising ego-death
by way of fusion with an energy that offers only
Destruction, beautiful as she is, so utterly complete
it echoes through time to pluck you from the point of
Inspiration, leaving a wanting void so clean this plane of
existence
shines all the more for not having known your rainbow stain
of desire?

Breathe. Just breathe.

Night Out

Good God, we're really on fire tonight.
There might not be anything left but
soot and ash in the morning, if there
even is a morning. Fuck, we're
really cooking tonight.

I'm not an astrology hack
but you could convince me
there's a celestial creep upon
the world tonight, some shadow
denouement cast by the fitting finale
of a forgotten fable concerning lost grace.

We're cooking. Fire in the veins,
flavor of iron on the tongue-
Nothing burns quite like
a crisp cool night with
rumors running round
that the sun is lying
dead in an alley
somewhere.

We're done for.
Finally.
Praise be.

I was so bored.

We're done for.

Praise be.

Finally.

Sunshine

A bitter tone seems to have settled
into the air as we slept
and I wake now to find
an army of anxieties marching
along the landscape of my mind

Dread-filled trenches carve up
the lining of my throat,
so I struggle to keep my lips
clamped shut lest their apocalyptic
contents spill over and
muddy the immaculate serenity
lying beside me

As I stare at the bedroom ceiling,
I meditate on the concept
of time travel and listen to
The Knocks of Morning Doom
at the front door

There is no escape,
for yesterday was this day
and tomorrow too, I will be
The-Man-I-Was-Last-Night-This-Morning
until until until

An Inch to the Left

I said, _My fingers are snakes_
and your face is a vulture.
You slipped a slice into
your mouth and asked
What does it mean?

I told you I wasn't sure
and that it came
to me on one of those nights
when everything in the world
felt exactly one inch to
the left of   normal.

You told me, _Snakes_
swallow eggs
and spit back
out the shells
And my eardrum
began to do that
thing where it
throbs to the tune
of Blue Monday.
What does it mean?

We may speak in our

familiar code and
kiss in a language
of solace but I still dream
of mausoleums and wake
to a dark figure
in the corner, cypher
in hand.

I write these words
one pronged tongue
flick at a time while it
watches, pecking
at the stolen finger
length, begging to know   *What does it mean?*

Run Boy Run

My dog passed. This was months ago.
Without warning, for a little while, the world ended.

We'd found each other in a dark park one night. He had
scabs all over his face.
Later, he'd on occasion find me in a pile of vomit. I had scabs
all over my past.

This dog ate up my affection. He rewarded it with immense
loyalty.
But he was his own worst enemy.
When he wasn't completely occupied loving me, he wanted
to tear little innocent things apart.
I think if anyone took too short of a look at him, they'd say
he was better off dead.

So, you see. We were the same.

He would have nightmares
that would make him cry in his sleep.
I would wake up clawing at my own skin.
I think for us both, morning brought with it
remorse for acts better left in our dreams.

So, you see. We were the same.

Taking him for walks was a herculean task in both strength and patience.

This beautiful, kind dog would disappear. All that would be left was pain and anxiety.

It was as if the world had sent to me a living representation of my ailments.

Or, at least, something to project them upon.

There was no reaching him. The most horrible howl would erupt from his throat and wear on my soul.

The force of the leash would tear at my bicep.

We would both be in a frustrated fury.

I dreaded those exercises in futility.

I'd rather we stay home.

I was in a fever back then. The adderall prescriptions would run dry days after refill.

The cocaine stopped being a party favor and was developing into a daily vitamin.

She worked night-shifts. So did my demons. And my dealer.

This dog would nip at my hands as I slipped out the door.

He didn't know. He couldn't. And yet, he did.

He'd rather I stay home.

So, you see. We were the same.

We tried everything.
I tried group therapy. He tried supervised play dates.
I tried cessation medication. He tried Prozac.
I tried switching to weed. He tried cbd pills.
I got a psychologist. He got a canine behaviorist.
Nothing really changed but the expectations of the people
we love.

Alas, there was one thing.
When I was at my best: I was a runner.
And there were times when on the leash, at a fast jog,
his storm may not have calmed
but seemed capable of focus.

So, I bought him a special harness
and this ridiculous leash
which strapped around my waist
in a way that reminded me of rappelling
in basic training all those years ago.
Inevitably, we appeared as we truly were:
misfits who had done away with all pretenses,
finally making corporeal the codependent
relationship tethering us together.

We would run like this through the nights.
Full heat. No sense of measure anywhere in our DNA.
Why would there be when it was just me and him?

There was no one around for us to pretend.
We could just be what we were:
Convicted hurricanes.
Natural disasters serving
time in mortal bodies.

For once, there was no howling.
No wailing in the dark.
He was unbridled light.
I was his comet's tail.

In those moments, as he pulled me faster than I'd ever run
before or since
-never indicating that for a moment he was ready for it to
end-
when our hearts were pounding and lungs dying,
we were finally just man and dog, boy and pup,
finding their step together.

When I could take no more, I'd reel him in.
He would walk by my side at a leisurely pace.
We were at peace.

These running dates made it harder to get high.
He would keep me sober that way.
Not always. But most of the time.

He wasn't perfect.
All his problems did not wash away.
Neither did mine.
But we had our moments that were just our own, in the night.
After my walk home past the street dealers and beckoning mistakes.
We had our moments racing in the night.

Then one day he couldn't run. Or play. Or eat.
Thousands of dollars of tests for a diagnosis of "unknown cancer."
In his last weeks, he would gather the energy to venture out.
But only ever so gingerly.

These walks were in the light of day.
In the light where I could see him wasting. Shaking. Scared.
Wondering what he did to deserve the pain he was in.

He was still a pup when I found him in that park. So I shared my birthday with him.
We were three years old when he got sick.
Then, one day, we weren't anything at all.

So, you see. I'm not the same.
But sometimes…

Sometimes, I try to feel for him in the nothingness he left in
his wake
and I find him in that secret space between reality and need,
blissfully ignorant of his weight upon me.

There are times that is enough to keep me straight. There are
times it isn't.

But mostly...
Mostly, I just run.

Nightshift

My girlfriend came home from her
nightshift, less than enthused
with my bodily state and story.
I must've tasted like molly and hate.
I decided, as we sat in the theatre
the next day, I truly loved her
although, I had been saying it for months.

To the Day

I was working that job: the one driving around
the rich guy and those test tube babies of his
he liked to swap out like designer handbags.

This was five years ago to the day, when life was strange.

You were a nurse on tinder: respectably high
off edibles when you swiped right and promised
you'd stitch me up at night if I decided to fight crime.

This was five years ago to the day, when life was carefree.

Hurricane Joaquin was rolling into town and the
entire city couldn't find it in them to give a damn.
We made plans to meet at midnight in this dive-bar
whose signature cocktail went by the name of ass-juice.

This was five years ago to the day, when life was cheap.

Joaquin was outside doing his best to leave a lasting
impression while I, two ass-juices deep, did the same.
Your future bridesmaid, assured I wasn't a serial murderer,
busied herself fending off deadbeats- leaving us to shout in
each other's ear the names of our favorite podcasts while
Dio (or Chopin, for all I know) played on the jukebox.

This was five years ago to the day, when life was surreal.

As our cab driver took a seventy dollar detour I was
nervous my overdraft couldn't cover, I leaned over
and kissed you (signaling to Joaquin our legacies was secure)
before returning to our conversation: the one that has yet to
end.

This was five years ago to the day, when life was just
beginning.

A Field of Study

On the morning of our wedding,
I wrote for you a letter
addressing the cosmic nature of
the curvature
of your ass...

As I await the university to review
my dissertation
on the matter and award me a
(most inevitable) PHD
for my work...

I have been horrified to discover
that marriage has
changed me and now nothing quite
makes me yearn
for you like...

The way you passionately
tell the Alexa
to go fuck herself.

Love Craft in the Time of COVID

It's only been a few days since the world decided to dabble in the latest fad diet: apocalyptic dread. It's only been a few days but she's somehow already finished a book. I, on the other hand, have picked up and put down no less than three. She splashes teaspoons of sauvignon blanc into each of our glasses while we cook. If she wasn't here, I'd have cracked open a beer before noon. She called her father. I pressed my nose to the window. She cleaned some corner of our one-bedroom I didn't know existed. I absorbed some useless fact about an unsolved murder in the 1970's.

I said the wine was for when we cook but I can't cook. She cooks. I watch and talk her ear off. We've found I'm good for exactly one thing in the kitchen: handling the raw meat. A little salt. Pepper. I have a talent for this. The messy part.

Still other times, we cook another way. She toils and I read to her. Neruda. Lovecraft. Ovid. Poe. Whatever catches my eye that hour. She says nothing when my heavy tongue demolishes some divinely structured sentence. Just keeps stirring or sautéing or whatever magic she does that inevitably sets off our apartment's lone smoke alarm. I give each character their own voice or accent and she laughs a laugh that convinces me it's just for her. I file it under the list of things I'll one day dwell on in my deathbed: us cooking.

We're watching another movie or show now. I'm laying out multiple theories about the ending. I'm talking like I know whodunnit. I've concocted and shared with her the means of guilt for every character, so how could I not? I cite my sources: glaringly obvious influences on the director. She listens attentively knowing damn well my predictions rarely pan out. This is how we watch. All the words and thoughts bursting out of my mouth, ears, and nose like streams syphoning directly from Narcissus's pool. This is how we are; this is how she lets me be. For too long it has been too good. An apocalyptic cocktail: made one part agony, two part ecstasy. The impending sense of doom making it all the more sweet.

My joy -never pure -is bookended with fear. My face occasionally flushes with fury at the thought of it all coming to an end, an anxiety of mine much older than any pandemic. I've never been one to wait for a crisis to dip my toe into the well of despair. I've been trained to expect the worst. For other boots to come falling when something feels just a bit too perfect. It feels like we've been living on borrowed time from the jump.

Now, she's telling me about workplace tribulations, trivial and otherwise. Moral obligations she runs into on her day to day. I listen, nod, and repeat back to her bits of pieces to show her I'm paying attention. That's difficult for me to do. It always has been. It was supposed to get better with age but yet here I stand at thirty years old. If it doesn't put my heart rate above 160 or have a plot, observing the world around me becomes a little like watching a washed out VHS tape. You've played it so many times that you get the gist of what's going on but the details are ultimately lost.

But when she speaks, I try. I really try. Sometimes I have to take a few seconds. Play back everything she just said to me in my head before I can process it all. And when the mental record button wasn't hit in time, I let her know. She might sigh but she never complains. Just calls me something so foul you'd be surprised she knew what it meant. Through my laughter, I try to press record once more but probably fuck it up. Not for the last time tonight, she starts to repeat herself.

I always try to give her a fix. Problem, meet solution. That's what I do. I'm a problem solver. But I'm aware that's not what she wants, that isn't why she's sharing. She knows that I know that isn't what she wants. But it's how I show her she's been heard. I think once I told her "Whatever decision you make will be the right one. You know, by default." At least, I hope I did. Let's say I did. These pieces I write are but one version of our reality. A momentary perspective distilled in some form that our grandchildren can read and unfairly compare their future relationships to.

"Whatever decision you make will be the right one." I hope I said that. It sounds like something that should be said to someone like her. So, let's say I did.

She makes more money than me and I brag about it to anyone that will listen. It's annoying. Even rude. But I can't get enough of how many of my peers seem uncomfortable with the very idea of it. Fuck it. I hate sports and swapping war stories at work can get old fast. Especially our war stories. It makes me feel elite. Progressive. Very east coast.

Her job is inarguably more important than mine. On my absolute best days, I get to be there for someone. Make them feel safe. Most days are not my best days. But her? She's there for not just one but many. She helps to stave off death. Or make the journey down the river styx less lonesome. She's battling actual elemental forces.

I always loved a good story. And that? That is the stuff of legend.

I used to think she didn't carry the weight of it all with her but it just took me a bit of time to see how she packed it. Just like with everything else, she does it neatly and with intention. It's saved for when there is proper time to parse through it all. I'm in awe of it, really. I grew up with happily married parents. A dog. Absolutely no childhood trauma. And yet, without so much as a warning I can find myself stepping into a bar and drinking myself into oblivion. For what? Because a few guys I knew once (and barely liked) killed themselves? Or maybe just because it's been too good for far too long again? The bar tab can't be paid by a handful of good reasons but it turns out they like VA disability pay just fine.

But not her. Not her.

She watches people die. And I don't just mean the part where their life ends. To truly watch someone die is to watch them struggle. Grasp. To let slip. Not go quietly. She watches them do their last living. And I can barely get this woman drunk on date night.

I am a mess and she is, very exquisitely, not.

That isn't to say she doesn't break. She does. We all do. But she does it in the way I have tried so hard to learn. She comes home and falls apart beautifully. Gracefully. All she asks for is an audience. While she lets slip. Let's go, quietly. She just needs me to watch her do some living. And to learn.

Tonight is our last night together before we're forced to share each other with the world again. We're on a video call with a myriad of friends that were once just mine but are now as eternally hers as I am. In the seconds between seconds, the secret spaces that I've learned to live in, I think about the stark contrast of what the coming weeks hold for us. She'll be on the frontlines and I'll be out there. Running around with my head cut off, solving small problems or possibly advancing the systemic oppression of entire classes of people. I haven't quite figured out which yet. There can be long periods of time where what I do is meaningless. Those days are when it's hardest to follow her example- to simply exist outside the tempest. I am not who she is. I am not even who she needs me to be. I am next to her now as I was truly born to be: raw and needful.

For so long, I approached the world as if I was a man prone to addiction and our life together suffered for it. It was only when I realized that I was but an addict pretending to be a man that we truly began to thrive. I ache for meaning. She bathes in it. I forage for relevance in the crevices of our pantry and in the muck along our fire escape. She wakes up as its heir apparent. I will spend my life outrunning uselessness. She will not ever know its cold embrace. She cannot fathom the impossibility of the metamorphosis her companionship demands of me by merely sharing our couch. I have never felt so humbled. So in love.

An errant hand smacks a container full of chocolates on the carpet just as we start to eat them. She strings together a litany of derogatory epithets that fill me with pride. I try to match her in creativity.

She doesn't hear a word of it over her own laughter.

Fuck-Ups and Foliage

The last time I was drunk
I shit in a garden
I strongly believe can be
found in the Financial District.

I told my wife I
wanted a divorce.
I told my wife I
planned to get high.
I told my wife I
would no longer
pay for her school,
which is a funny thing,
because I do not do that.

The last time I was drunk
was the last time, but
the last time before that
I vomited in a cab and
used my runner's legs
to flee the scene and
my dignity.

The first time I drank
for the last time,

I drove my car into a
melon farm and searched
the headlines to see if
I might have killed someone.

I have hands that
I truly believe
have helped to save lives
and keep people safe
but none of that changes the fact that…

The last time I was drunk
I shit in a garden
I strongly believe can be
Found in the Financial District.

What Sounds Will You Haunt Me With?

So much of my love for you
Is expressed in
An internal language, built
Upon a lexicon deeply
Rooted in what I reluctantly
Imagine it will be like
To perhaps one day
Forever
Lose you

When we are together, content
And without crisis
To sublet our one bedroom, my
Heart reserves within it
A well of despair and develops
Upon it a film of worry
Over how this might
All come
To an end

Everytime you leave our fortress
Of solitude and matrimony,
-Mine Own Ragnarok-
Ephemeral whispers ask of me
What sounds you might choose

To haunt these narrow
But beloved halls with
If you were to
Never return

Will it be the clearing of your throat
Or some other innocuous action
That I am not yet aware
I could pluck out from the sea
Of all others in existence, such as
The sound of your wooden spoon
Slapping the side of my metal pot
Or will it be the satisfied chef's chirr
you don't know you make ?

Which will you use to steal
The air from my lungs and boil
The blood in my heart and cause
The gaping maw inside to gulp
Entire galaxies?

What sounds will you haunt me with
After we are torn apart and
We have both become spectres
Of our own fashion, languishing
In this world?

Summer Temptations

Where I come from, the sky
knew better than
to open mid-year,
interrupting my youth.

My mother and father
would never
stand for
The Dampening
of those walls
or the foundation
they stood on.

This city of mine
is slick and warm as
bathwater, always
daring me to
issue it orders, begging
me to humiliate myself
with acts of audacity
and agency.

In this city of mine,
the sky weeps with pleasure
and beckons

to back rooms, back thoughts
shutting doors and shattering
promises with the force
of Odinson.

These walls now creak
with age and whispers
of mutiny.

Tantamount

There's a subtext to all of this:
a view through a romantic prism lens
clutched like Comfort Come,
codified creation conforming
The Craft
from indulgent compulsion
to the spectacle
of bloodsport.

You would have me
act as Houdini in chains,
exorcising demons for show,
the both of us
coddled by the safety of the stage.

You would have me strip
bare the rage of revolution and rape
until all that is left is
tantamount to a
production of puppets on a stage.

You would have me
open my mouth and breathe
my tempest into your chest
as if I no longer held the need
to feel its stir in my own.

You would have me
murder all that I hold holy
because we both know
how long I have waited
to take this bow.

A Type of Writer

I want to buy a typewriter,
but not because I'm some
asshole who believes it represents
the only medium for my art,
that it's the one true instrument
of demonic synchronicity
between man and the promethean
gift of language.

I want to buy a typewriter
because they are quite heavy
and unlikely to be suspected as
a means or method of murder despite
the nations and peoples
to have met their end by way of
their satisfying
Klick-Klack Keystrokes..

I want to buy a typewriter
because I want to marvel
at the power to create and destroy
hiding in plain sight.
I want to buy a typewriter
to drop it on your damn head
when the revolution
(or maybe just Wednesday) comes along.

Blue Collar Poet

Pray tell,
what hopeless handful of hate
will you, racing the sun,
smear on script tonight
lest this dream be undone?

Will you finally
scrawl out success
where there is none
in protest of future imperfect
Kingdom Already Come?

Blue Collar Poet,
press your pen in
pained palm, your haunting
has only just begun—
persist now, we dance until
The Long Night is won

On Company Time

I want to set the sun like an old egg-timer.
I want to freeze the cosmic clock
with an omnipotent whistle or
perhaps a flip of the bird.
I want to tear a pocket universe from the
fabric of my living room
and declare it the Fortress of
Leave-Me-The-Fuck-Alone.

Give me an hour turned eon to
exist without rent,
read without hurry,
drink without stupor,
lounge without atrophy,
and fuck without distraction.

Give me divinity or give me death
because liberty alone
doesn't stand a chance against
the goddamn workweek.

About You

I used to think I would not write
about you as you never chose to
rattle the walls with tempestuous
rage nor did you bother to chill my
bones with protracted performances
of cold indifference

I used to think I would not write
about you as with your kiss came no
pain and your love- no cost
Your attention required no price
of admission and your presence
demanded not even an ounce
of my flesh

This was before I knew
the love sonnet could be
more than a desperate
plea in the face of the
Unrequited
This was before I knew
anguish did not hold
monopoly on strains of
Inspiration
This was before I knew

nirvana was hiding in
your eyes and
serenity in your hair,
both waiting to
ambush me-
Strip Me Bare

I used to think I would not write
about you and now I cannot
foresee the day your gaze
won't peer back at me from
behind every word, every line
calling me home

On Vows

My wife let me pick her
paint-by-numbers: the
portrait of a skull-faced
woman and a black cat.
She hates it.

It is gaudy as a
brooch-supernova
and one of my most
prized possessions.

I keep it in my office,
which coincidentally,
doubles as a bedroom corner.
While my bride sleeps,
I sometimes whisper across
the room to the witchy thing,
still wet with commitment.

"All of it," I say. "You
are proof she meant
all of it. Every word."

Edicts of Expectation

I've mapped these ley lines
for too many nights to just now
notice the neon incantation
hanging on the edge of the sky:
BEWARE.

If I had my way,
whispering useless tips
to tired dogs guarding
cities turned mausoleums
would be cardinal in nature
but, as it stands,
little legislation yet sprouts
from the mouths of boy-men
who still open magnetic doors
with telekinetic motions of the hand.

The truth is
my hackles tire of standing in wait
for the discovery of
rotten morsels of indication
these urban matrices may
finally resume their triumvirate reign
of the ripple-plex hedonism way.

And yet, she insists:
BEWARE.

A promise, I hope.

Dream-Girl

Though,
I can so often
be found by your side
I am quite aware that
you can interpret in my eyes
the methodical manner
by which
my mental meanderings
cast my attentions quite far,
cursing you
with the irony of
a man you can touch
yet on occasion
find nowhere at all.

Nevertheless,
upon my return
and without fail,
I find you awaiting
patiently the luminary
storm of words
I have inevitably
scraped off the surface
of some podunk used-up
dying daydream star

as though you suspect no
cascading supernova
below my feet
holds a candle to
the gravitational well
with which
our fusion demands
it compete.

Adagio

Come an age upon which the mind
can know everything and nothing
all at once,
the fertile terf of creation may find within itself the
infection of decay, a ripening bloom of the sinfruit.
We may then turn to the gateways of change,
-The Ancient Methods-
not for their truth (of which they boast so little) but
for the purity of the focused meditation on the mysteries,
the room they made for wonder in an age when the
contents of bottled elixirs were meaningless in the face of
the rituals in which they were imbibed, for
the negative tongues
we adopt in preparation
of the change in spirit
to come.

I do not take the sacrament.
I need no compass for daily prayer.
I stumble when my path is onefold, nevermind eight.
Yet, I have stared upon the eldritch face of that titanic
shrine for so many new dawns, I know I have felt the
kismetic beat make rise within me something true as truth
when the spheres dance across its precipice and only now
do I recognize the same power simmering in the

present air as when I was a child and
the figures on the sacred pages
had but one decree to issue:
Become What You Were Meant To Be

Slowly-
But surely.

Everyone's a Fucking Phoenix

We are all, apparently,
drowning in the residue
of warrior-cocoon-hatchlings
and my favorite jeans are
stained now with perseverance.
I don't see it coming out in the wash.

So many people have risen
from these fucking ashes
at this point, we should be checking
to see if there's some sort of
renewable energy source
underneath the pile.

I just coughed up a goddamn ember
of resurrection that was hiding
in my cheeseburger.
The patty is now aching
in newly transmogrified pain.

All I ask is if it's going to
make so much noise as I chew, perhaps
the
formerly-bovine-now-future-warrior-cocoon-hatchling
Phoenix

at least do me the favor of
finding a new metaphor to
describe the ways with which it
plans to reconstitute itself
from my shit.

Perhaps it could return as
one of those sewer alligators
we used to hear so much about.

Everyone's a fucking Phoenix.
No one's a goddamn gutter gator.

Plague

"I am so damn bored all the time,"
is too simple a way to announce
one's self as a burning effigy
of romanticized expectations.

And yet, here we are.

"Let's think of something
to do next week, maybe upstate,"
is the closest I can come to describing
the existential dread plaguing me.

And yet, it's all I have.

"Did I fuck everything up last
night or will you give me another chance?"
was the most honest thing uttered within
the confines of our little Shangri La.

And yet, you're still here.

Escape From Harlem

I hate the man on my stoop.
I don't hate him for being poor.
I don't hate him for being unconscious.
I don't even hate him for being a drug addict.
I hate him because he reminds me of myself.
I want him moved. I want him _re_moved.
I want him erased. I want to erase that part of _myself._
I want us both erased and then I want to be remade.
Without him on my fucking stoop.

Soon, I will flee. I will make my home between the Park and
Juilliard. My neighbor, Angel Moroni, will play his golden
trumpet atop his marble white church and in his grand
consideration of the neighborhood, will refuse to make a
sound. I will share a courtyard with the Museum of Folk Art.
With a wink, its staff will tell me they serve wine on
Wednesdays. It will be my concrete utopia.
There will be no one there for me to hate but myself.

Before I flee. Before the great escape to Urbanopia™. Before
Harlem. There was Bedstuy. Glorious Bedstuy. With its
friendly block parties. Its _good mornings_, its _have a blessed
day_s. Beautiful Bedstuy. With its French restaurants, vegan
bar food. Affordable backyards. Perfect Bedstuy. A
gentrification that you can stomach, that you can wash down
real nice with a growler of craft beer from the corner bar.
Where the cocaine and weed gets delivered in cars and stays
off the streets. Where the sex work waits until sundown, out

of respect. Where you can be hip and cool but, you know…
safe, baby.

And then comes Harlem. Because if you gotta move, you
gotta move somewhere with as much soul as Bedstuy. You're
not cut out for that cushy Manhattan, that plastic "Oh,
Daniel, will you call the elevator for me?" Manhattan. You're
here for the guts. You're here for the grit. You're here for the
adventure. You're here to have your ass kicked.

Maybe it was the dishwasher. It was probably the
dishwasher. I'd say it was definitely the dishwasher that
started it all. It wasn't broken. Okay, I broke it. But just the
plastic part. And I break a lot of things. That doesn't explain
the sewage that pushed its way up. The sewage no one could
explain how to stop from coming up. That doesn't explain
how you could slap new paint and new appliances atop
decades of neglect and demand a new beginning. So I'd say it
was definitely maybe the dishwasher that told me some soul
doesn't forget. Some soul aches more than other soul.

In Angry Harlem. No *good mornings*. No *have a blessed days*.
God minded his business in Harlem. In Raging Harlem.
Corner vegan restaurants close early while crime scene
analysts look for spent casings. In Vengeful Harlem. Where
you go for a run and find your window open wider than you
left it. Where the corner gets quiet when you walk by with
your light skin and short hair. Where someone takes the
dog's leash out of your fiancé's hand and says, "He's mine
now." Where you learn the *shame* of fear.

Maybe it was the crack. It was probably the crack. I'd say it was definitely the crack that really made me run. I was broken. Okay, I'm still broken. But I'm better now. And I've figured out how to be broken. That doesn't explain how I had memorized the face of every dealer on the block, men a quiet part of me was all too happy to see. That doesn't explain how my addict eyes had spotted which delis sold dollar pipes from behind the counter. So I'd say it was definitely maybe the crack that told me what I hated about Harlem was what I hated about myself. Some hate hurts more than other hate.

I hated watching the super chasing away the young woman trying to get high by the basement door.
I hated being the only one to notice the baggie
she left on the steps by the stoop.
I hated knowing what I did and did not do with it would be between only me and Frederick Douglass.

So, you tell your fiance, "Look, we gotta go." And she says, "Yeah, I know!" And even though it's only been ten weeks, you know there isn't a choice. You remind yourself that you used to live in Bedstuy™. You tell yourself you're hip to the socioeconomic basis of what you're experiencing and it's not fear packing those boxes, it's *fucking capitalism, man!* You tell yourself that you know your experience isn't all experiences and that you won't let the hate and fear take root, you won't fall prey to that particular rot. But you know. You know you're going to take a long look at that crime map before you choose your next spot. You know when you go to sign that next lease, you'll have a fresh shave and find a way to mention where you work and where you have worked. You know if you were asked to, you would scrub the melanin right the fuck out of your last name while the landlord nods approvingly. You know that it's your white fiancé with a 999 credit score that seals the deal.

And then comes the West Side. Because if you gotta move again, you gotta move where there's no soul. Or even soul™. Turns out you *are* cut out for that cushy Manhattan, that plastic "Oh, Jan, how is your little Pekingese?" Manhattan. You're here for the glitz. You're here for the glam. You're here for the safety, environment, education, and infrastructure. You're here because you have the luck, the means, the privilege and you know exactly where you would be if you didn't.

Angry Raging Vengeful Harlem,
I hated the unconscious man on my stoop because that man was me waiting to be.
You deserve more than some troubled transplant trampling the sands of Black Galilee.

On Patience

Out the window of this bus I can see the Empire Hotel
followed shortly by the Empire Bar
which comes just before the Empire Szechuan
found right across the street from the Empire Man,
who, night after night, dances his Empire Body
in the dark just blocks from the Juilliard School of Empire Arts
as though he came to dance for its Empire Eyes
and found its Empire Doors
closed to him, yet refused to be dismissed because these Empire Lands

find their borders cease with
the down of our brown skin
because our hearts
beat renegade red
and our smiles still
remember the cocoa kisses
of lovers past in
the twilight times of Montezuma:
who's demise remains our eternal
promise of the inevitability of the eclipse
and constant reminder that no matter
how high the monuments
or how fervent the prayer
even the most mighty of
domains must meet an Empire's End.

<u>The View From 112th</u>

A planet hangs above the
Dark Geometry of St. John's
as Sol rises in the distance,
dragging with it a begrudged morn
and the twilight of my watch with it.

There's a sense of divinity to the
scene, the likes of which we
might imagine igniting
Young Keats into an explosion
of foundational romance.

Perhaps I, too, will lay down
my vocation and life to
walk away from this world
in favor of what beauty may come.

White Hot

Reaching out across the abyss
like a poor man's Kwisatz Haderach,
I try to feel what he feels by
forcing myself through
the masochistic trial
of fathoming
his loss.

All I can conjure is an echo
of rage, white hot and burrowing
its way through his every vein
like hungry lightning, leaving
gnawing claps of thunder
to demonstrate
an absence.

I slip on his pain like a darkly dyed
sleeve, and our every atom appears now
a Nagasaki, our every cell now
a Roanoke, and our every
breath a crime and every
moment alone an invitation
to the promised land
of Annihilation.

I want to shed this common skin
I want to rid myself of burden
I want to mind my business
I want to ignore my gut
I want to not know
what I know
I know.

Tomorrow we take his guns.

Big Apple Leftovers

This city never sleeps?
It tires of all the bullshit
like anyone else, I promise.
Our midnight souls
looking for romance
in alleyway kingdoms
are no more than the rodents
searching for purpose
in sewer grate elysiums.
It's all just an ecosystem
refusing to acknowledge
our existence.

New Sensation

This isn't meditation.
This isn't prayer.
This isn't poetry in the tea garden,
moonlight on the veranda or
harmony in the heart.

This is something darker:
lamentations spelled out in raised skin,
cryptids whispering from forrest lines
and long calculating fingers
with no known origin-
beckoning.

What these shut eyes see and this
starship-body perceives is a velocity
outracing all things terminal,
string theory bending to a divine strum
upon a bass instrument at the
acoustic heart of consciousness.

What's happening here has no name.
What's happening here cannot end.
What's happening here feels like
Genesis but has the
tell-tale vibrations
of Annihilation.

We Can Be Poets

It doesn't have to be like this:
all chakras and empowerment,
good vibes and dead-faced lies.
You don't have to film yourself
pretending to write
in a field of flowers.

It doesn't have to be like this.
All peppermint and pumpernickel,
whatever that is.
It can be rock, roll, and
the guillotine-n-between.
You can shoot an apple off your
wife's head and sometimes miss.

Our predecessors drank themselves
to death and called it art
like the mastercraft liars they are,
grifting to the bitter end
as they stuck their heads in the oven.

We're con-artists, thieves, and thugs.
The flyting founders
bled each other
to death for fun

with the shiv of a well-placed
word and the cut of blackscratched page.

We don't have to be life-coaches.
We can be rogues and revolutionaries.
We can be journalists sending dispatches
from the frontlines of Hell.

We can be poets.

A Growing Burden

Predators stick to the night
not because of any romance
or inky anonymity
hidden in the cool air
but for in the glow
of day, glass and water
conjure reflections-
With sunlight comes
guilt.
With sunlight comes
reckoning.
With sunlight comes
a world that left
the jungle
behind.

The Foliage Rebellion

There is upon us a changing of order
when from the chaos of summer air
blooms a semblance of discipline
as gravity resumes the reigns
of reality and the anarchist plumage
that had reared its head in
a fit of spring naivete
meets its inevitable end on the
Killing Floors of the Autumnal Nation.

<u>*Illustrative*</u>

Without warning, my eyes-bewildered
gazed male upon my body-unassuming,
finding it blighted by tumors
sprouting from genetic soil rich
in surprise and resentment,
my skin postured and lamented,
scarred with intent yet boasting no purpose,
as though I had just emerged from bathing
in the warm waters of Lake Toxicity itself,
before laying down upon the mud of masculinity.

My reflection seceded
from childish fantasy
and brought my
unwilling attention
to the black ink script
dripping down my back
in languages I cannot speak,
spelling out passages from books
I have not read, illustrating
my jungle familiars according
to systems of belief I do not subscribe to.

Just more examples,
I concluded,

of battle scars from a war
no one asked me to fight.

The Schtick

To My Toxic Masculinity,

I am
so tired of
this "Last Cowboy" act
of yours. You are exhausted
from the constant need to keep
your heartbeat pounding. A junkie
in the truest sense of the word, you
don't even know how to begin to want
to stop. You are not Samurai. There are
no such things as heroes and this world will
be better off when your whole schtick finally accepts
extinction. Adapt. Change. Grow. Or it will cost you your
life.

Sincerely,
Your Weary Body

Echoes

As the tempest dithers,
losing motive and power
to the creeping calm
infecting its manic winds
like leperous limbs,
phantom pleas of future ghosts
(the past fails to forget)
may be heard as the sea of progress
swallows them whole.

Pay them no mind.
The sun sets on thee and thee alone.

Demigod

I tire of telling people
I'm the chosen one
and having them asking
who's doing the choosing
like there's some rule
against second comings
drugging and boozing.

Trust me, hear me out.
I know what you're thinking
I'm not going manic any more
than Augustine in his moment
of moral panic.

Let me just lay it out
my future state
literary caliphate,
No need for an iron-fist
I'll rule by brilliance in verse
the sort of thing to outlive
any journey ending in a hearse.

Have you your doubts?

No worries, just read my words:
feel the drip drip drip

of ambrosia leaking
from my fingertip-
I've got the pantheon's attention,
Aphrodite looking in the
dedication for a mention.
It's in my words you'll find
the limerence you seek
when past the cosmic curtain
you take a lysergic peek.

Krypton Clarity

Breaching this
Alternate Dimension Come,
one discovers it lays claim
to a sunrise
in which the ultraviolet rays
hold no sting of pain
and the morning dew
boasts no flavor of shame.

Breathing in
an alien atmosphere
of forgiveness, old strength
returns anew to muscle
no longer straining to bear
simian loads, the steady
hum of Bardo now
sounding a tune less sinister.

Dreams now
unburdened by the
weight of penance find
they fly higher than
their guilt-ridden fathers ·
ever imagined from the safety
of their doomed planets.

The Still

I've spent my youth
looking, looking
for orgasmic ascension in
euphoria bombs capped upon
endorphin packed epiphany rockets.

All I've ever wanted was
to shred reality
to pieces for the high-crime
of being found too silent
for far too long and
I never could quite resist
making ripples and waves
with my boredom-born fists.

Alas, I know now
it is finally time to find
the serenity in the still-
So, I begin the ritual
of cuffing my wrists with
the silver of restraint because
the golden rule for this bronze boy
has always been: _Mind the Idle Hands._

Self-Defense

When you have been
training for the coming
of a new day
for what feels like eons,
Sensei, Sifu, Guru,
begin to both blend
together and fade away,
leaving only the art of living:
The Kata,
The Kung Fu,
The New You,
staring at the old.

Dare it to make the first move.

Precarious

"Do I have to worry about you?"

I am in the precarious situation
of not having had to lie to you
in so long, the scent of the question
gives me more pause than
the taste of an absent answer.

The truth and the lie both
fill out the same figure,
split the same silhouette,
endebt the same flesh, so it is no wonder:
they filet my face in much the same way.

My greatest shame is how well
I've conditioned you to see my
skin crawl even before the
rot finds its way to the rind.
My greatest weapon in this war is
the beat of fear I taught your heart
the rhythm to.

"Do I have to worry about you?"

Like a draw-string on some vintage
action hero figurine
you pull to feel safe,
I sound my line with the authenticity
of the laugh-tracks that kept me
late-night company as a child
and usher you off to bed hoping
I've awarded you the same comfort.

As you watch me walk into the dark to feel for
the midnight pulse in
the moon-knight sheen,
my shoulders long vacant of influence
and my head heavy with hope
you have to know,
    you have to know,
        you have to know

                        for the both of us.

<u>The Three-Poison Coven</u>

I am
fighting for the future in which
the devil-shaped door leading
to my heart isn't left ajar
by Ignorance, Desire, and Aversion
as they sing their
come-hither hymns
and cast their midnight spells,
summoning familiar lowlight hells.

Drought

The stagnant tremor of The Still
permeates the tectonic relation
between each moment.
This cancer takes root,
reigns, rips, & razes
your precious hold on The Now.
The curse of an end
perpetually nigh
assures a smile spread upon
your licked-chapped lips
though, your
battle-brazed brain has not felt
the drench of a berserker's bath
since the age of fantasy dried up
along with all the oceans
and other pleasantries
this world once had to offer like
Rhythm & Reason.

The Point

Of late, the words spilling from my lips
have alluded to the pagan significance
of conditions believed necessary to put
pen to paper.

These illicit murmurs signal
planetary alignments, instructing me to
delineate preordained points of rendezvous
in the twilight dimensions whereupon
I will touch God- scraping free
a piece of sacred flesh for my
own dark designs.

Yet even as I partake in such
delicious dalliances with inspiration
I think of the these chthonic meetings
and the warnings whispered wherein:
This world does not end in fire
but with fingertips wet
with the dew of a dream
just out of reach.

Give Them My Best

The best writers must be orphans
what with their lackadaisical
romps through time, care-free
razing of reputations
flaunted in the
face of fear.

The best writers must be lowmen
who need not make whispers
about discretion or propriety as
they zip up their mongrel souls
and sweep broken hearts under
motel bed frames

The best writers are the best writers
for they answer only to their
midnight selves, the destroyers
within acting only on appetite,
enjoying baptism in the
freedom of abandonment

The Tournament

When I write, I do so as if
I were seated at a roundtable
alongside challengers
most deadly, peers
both beloved
and despised-
Romantic androids:
bastards, all of them.

When I write
it's with everything to prove,
the jaws of irrelevance
snapping at my heels and
the safety net of delusion
well-frayed from overuse.

Commercial souls write their
words of kindness which,
in full indoctrinated spirit,
are not far from the grasp
of learned machines.
However, my back breaks
itself into this arch
out of malice, drunk on calm
confidence *I am no replicant.*

I'm not writing to live
or earn your love.
I'm writing to kill you
and your hive-mind dreams,
I'm writing for the world
to come hither
so that I might swallow it whole.

Working Title
(with Akimbo)

Searching under the floorboards of my mind
for loose change literary references
I can spend on spiritual anecdotes
draped in capes stitched of stories,
hymns of relationships past
lining the pockets with mundane musings
I'll need back in the morning
I want to pull at existential threads
dyed dread-red and woven into sarcasm

Dancing around the obvious
I pack harmless flirtations into cigarette shaped boxes
letting out smoke signals carrying compliments
I hope these miscast spells and clumsy hexes act as
Valkyries of innocence and interest

Reckoning this exchange as the mobius
that bands us together in a world gone silly
I claim my worth figurative, value metaphysical
may this be the harbinger of who I'm meant to be

exploit.exe

We are not the same.
Yes, poetry is in everything
but everything is not poetry.
As with any witchcraft,
the magic manifests from intent.

We are not the same.
We may trade in similar goods
as our products are indeed made
up of both language and experience,
but I am a craftsman studying his art,
challenging his limits to duels,
struggling to keep afloat
in a river of monotony
as a school of barracuda-anxieties
nip at my raw heels.

You are the MegaCorp retailer,
engineered for algorithm
maximization and mass production.
Your words, knowing neither agony
nor lust, have never made the
acquaintance of your artistic integrity.

But I, but I, but I…
I am a Prince of the Universe: Storyborn,
Bard Assumptive, student of
the wordjammer way.
The Real-Deal Reincarnate.

We are not the same.
You would rule this world.
But I, but I, but I…

Traditions

When I am old,
happily dying next
to you or perhaps
horribly alive and well
and alone…

I will remember with longing
Saturday mornings
when my only
title in the world was 'Husband'
and my only task that mattered
was buying the loaf of
San Francisco sourdough from the
Manhattan Farmer's market for la
Mansión Familiar masquerading as a
one-bedroom, one-bath
in the city.

Brown Like Me

I have no community.
To many I am
an avatar of erasure.
Coconut, they'll label me.
Brown on the outside,
white on the inside.
Not a real mexican.

I stand alone, born with
my native tongue
already cut from my mouth
and yet still,
they seek to rob me,
annex the spark within
so that everything of worth
is still muddied by
the brand of assimilation.
They'll say I am
one of the good ones.

I am nowhere to be found
on the silver screen or pale page.
The token character's accent
sounds unfamiliar and
la vieja on the street
shakes her head in pity
as her beautiful language
paints my face
the color of loneliness.
Una pena, she says.

I steal strength from solitude:
the scion of a New Breed.
All that I have, all that I bring
is mine and mine alone.
I am nobody's *good one.*
My mastery and shame
acknowledge no cultural empire.
I claim them in my name as
no one can be brown
quite like me.

Vintage

My twenties were easier
to swallow, good for the
digestion even.
I keep a bottle of the stuff stashed.

The color of my mayhem
used to be more pleasing
to the eye.
We used to paint the streets with it.

And my stories, my stories
would keep me warm in
the cold winds of regret.
Now, that manuscript is
too wet with shame and pride
to ever catch so much
as a single
spark.

Growth

I found myself tired
of acting a bastard,
so I grew upon my face
a thin veneer of
my father
and was shocked to discover
Gods and other
Grifters of Joy
to be far less fickle than
when I used to spend my days
bathed in midnight oil,
walking about the streets
asking for a match.

Mark of the Tide

Snow swept affairs born
in the bosom of blizzards
bleed away to nothing,
nothing more than
blemishes on a playlist
as the mortar sets
between the bricks on
this house, our house-
built to last through minor
Acts of God and major
Acts of Me.
Tell them, tell them all
the halfkind lie:
that I've learned, learned
How To Be.

Spring is coming,
The Tide is coming,
My Mind is coming.
So, let us wait and see.

Genesis Rejected

It always starts with,
'In the beginning…
as if there existed such a thing.

They seek to make you finite,
adrift in an endless kismetic sea.
The Titans. Ptah. Yahweh.
All Ones. Great Ones. First Ones.

But it is you, The Reader,
who is above and before all,
aglow in enlightenment
with the knowledge that all things
to be have already been.

The age of subjugation cedes
to the dawn of your perception
of the cycle of expansion and retraction:
Eternal Baptism found
in the concept of universal heat death.

The era of empowerment is
awakened by the epoch of
of one's own gleaning.

Wield the deification of self
as Slave Liberated, Consciousness
Ascended, and Ego Annihilated.

The Past is before us, awaiting formation.
The Future is now, lamenting your coronation.
The Present is your kingdom, awaiting reign sublime.

Elucidate

I'm working a case,
chasing a lead, and
I have commissioned a sketch
of the suspect in question:
my fugitive blue-collar mantra,
the coyote smuggler who will finally
lead me to The Nirvanic State
whose citizenship allows
for immigrants with
little more to offer than bodies
chipped and frayed,
undone by dreams less so lost
than quietly unmade.

Resistance

At the feet and mercy
of some eldritch horror,
the integrity of my
creative nation-state (and
its body politic) both
bow and strain under
the pressure of this titan
spun out from
the bloat of space and time.

It has a name.

Something ancient
now slithers
where dream once dwelt.

And it has a name.

<u>*Not in the Dark*</u>

Time with myself is dangerous. It's like being a child without parents. I let myself do whatever I want. Wake up at five o' clock in the morning to drink coffee and watch a Scorsese film?
Go for it.
Sleep in till noon and play video games?
Be my guest.
Work out as soon as possible so we can have a drink earlier?
So we can brush our teeth and drown the scent with mouthwash earlier.
So we can make the decision to relapse earlier.
Give us more time to shake that old coke tree, see what falls out of the dealer's pockets.
Do it.

I am a prisoner. I am a free and wild man that has built a gilded cage around himself with all the things he loves. I have installed guards at all the gates.

Correctional officers take the form of my wife and friends, rattling the bars of my cage at night.
"Are you okay? Talk to me. Just promise you'll call before you use again."
Best not catch you sleeping, Dog. We know what your dreams look like.
Badadadada. Badadada.

I like to feel good. Then better. Then like a god. Not God. But just a god. Like a thing capable of divinity but too cool for it. I wear white T-shirts and tight jeans. James Dean. But with a family. And 401k.

And that is the problem, isn't it? I want to be a beast one day. And a family man the next. I want to call my mother but I want to fuck like a bastard. I want to cook breakfast with my wife but I also want to be allowed to sleep off the coke and whiskey until there's no headache to wake up to. I have surrounded myself by all that I love and become too constricted to be this thing I so badly want to be.
Rejoice.

When I die they will say I was a good man. That's because no one ever shows up to talk about what a son of a bitch you are. Maybe someone drinks to that privately somewhere, but they don't show up to make a show of it.
Rejoice.

There's decency in the world yet.
Perhaps, not in the dark.
But that's why we hold our funerals during the day.

They will say of me, he was a good man because look at all these good things he did. He was there for me. He was there for them. His heart yearned to help so many. But there will be those who know the piece of shit that I was, too. And they will keep that to themselves because at least I was their piece of shit.

There will be a war between what some knew me to be and what others knew I was capable of. There will be hushed battle amongst those that deem me worthy of remembering one way. Or the other. Was he a good man or a creep? He was both and neither. *Who were we talking about?*

There will be solitude and solace eternal only in being quickly forgotten.

But what if I could be something else. What if I could be something so irrefutable that no revelation could pry it from the grasp of my cold dead hands.

What if I was a writer? What if I was absolved not by redemptive acts or confession but by the merit of my craft. What if I was a writer? What if I was heard and pondered and valued and validated. What if I was immortal? All could be forgiven. Or held against me. But at least I would be… *At least I would be.*

Samsara

Leaving a screaming path
along the thoughtstream dimension,
phenomena recurs, establishing itself as habit:
a gaping maw forms where the soul should reside,
attempting to supplicate itself with the spice of spiritus
mystici.

And yet the Empire of Impermanence reigns eternal,
outlasting ouroboran feasts, the fever of a dragon's desire,
even the preponderance of piety amongst midworld deities.

Death I have become.
Life I have arrived.
The Beauty lies in the between.

In the The Garden of Transition,
the last bastion of familiarity
to flourish under such darklight rays,
wake where the dew of origin forms
and rest in the twilight of demise.

Find me in the between.

Acknowledgements

The acknowledgments page is an interesting test of my self-discipline, an attribute which I was not born with a natural predilection for. My initial instinct with any creative task is to subvert expectations, to walk the road of what has become before and hook a hard left when those following along might least expect it.

That's it really. That's my creative formula. The secret sauce is in fact just mayo and ketchup, you know? The trick is, in the singular case of the acknowledgements page, is to be self-aware enough to know there is nothing creative about gratitude.

In life, I have used hedonism and humor alike to shield myself against harsh realities but the act of giving thanks must remain sacrosanct in its emotional vulnerability. Quite simply, when it comes to this one thing: _I cannot fuck around!_

So, let's get to it.

There is no doubt as to where to begin this round robin of appreciation. I'd like to thank my darling wife, Petra, without whom I would not be typing this today. She is the one who initially weaned me off an addiction (among others) to pouring my writing energies into long, fraught reddit comments. She has read countless versions of most of the content in this book, proving that her patience is a bottomless well. At my lowest points in life, this woman has continually picked me up off the floor, shook me out, and said "You've still got your best days ahead of you." I love her dearly and in many ways, every word I write is for her.

Next up, we have my amazing parents, Karen and Russell, who walled our home with books of all sorts. When our modest collection wasn't enough to satiate the appetites of my sister and I, these patron saints of literacy allowed us to haul back books by the wagon load from the Sunnyvale Public Library. All of this might have led to the creation of an avid reader, but I have to credit my father for driving me toward my first fix of a writing high. Catching me in a fit with rage born of some slight by a school friend, he suggested I find some paper to write down how I felt instead of taking the skinny kid next door by the arm and twirling him around like I had done in times previous. I never really put down that pen and to this day, I credit him with the rarity with which I fling rude children about.

A special thanks must then also be directed toward my sister, Nicole, who publicly accused me of having plagiarized my first poem. That, Dear Reader, is when I first knew I *really* had something.

I would like to thank my friend, the incredibly talented Tiffany Lin, a prolific artist currently serving as a Professor at the University of Nevada, Las Vegas. It was Tiffany who suggested I write a submission for her mango themed art exhibition: *AT THE PITH* hosted by the Nook Gallery in Oakland, California. My essay "Exotic Fruit" was first presented there and in many ways, that invitation was the genesis of *Speaking in Midnight Tongues*, so I am forever grateful to her for that invitation back into the waking world of art after all too long a hibernation. In the same vein, I would like to thank Catherine Whattam, the world's most natural born hype-woman and loyal friend, for pushing me to create @mileswrites on instagram, a platform that I may not always love but I heavily credit with igniting a flurry of work that formed this collection. A bit like a motivational version of Tom Joad, Catherine can be found wherever morale is low and belief in one's self is most needed. Just when you think there's nothing left for you to dream: she'll be there.

It was on that platform that I formed a very rewarding friendship with the Bombay based poet, Ankita Roy, who granted me permission to out her as the owner of the pen name *Akimbo* in this acknowledgement. Perhaps one of the most encouraging souls I have come across who truly understands the transcendent pain of obsessing over every singular word we've written but somehow still leaving room for typos, I am incredibly proud to display our collaborative piece, *Working Title*, in this book. You can find more of her atmospheric, exquisitely somber, and nostalgia-infused work at @akimbowrites on instagram.

I will keep my expression of gratitude for the secretive team at *The Void* magazine brief, as even acknowledging their existence might be a transgression against their fight club style rules. However, I would be remiss if I did not mention one of the most affirming experiences in my creative journey thus far was when they decided to publish *Escape From Harlem* in their November 2020 issue. That piece truly reached its greatest potential in no small part due to their editing team- in particular, the mysterious but frighteningly skilled Maggie. No last lame. Just Maggie. As I said, they're secretive.

I cannot overstate my profound appreciation for my friend and illustrator, Pedro Gomes, who created all art associated with this book. I came to this titan of talent without so much as a title and little more than a handful of screenshots of my work. Somehow from that molehill of direction, he created the thematically resounding mountain of creativity that is this book cover! I would not be anywhere near as proud of *Speaking in Midnight Tongues and Other Symptoms of Neon Fever* as I am without the degree of professionalism his art brought to the project.

There are always more to thank.

There are more worthy of dedications.

But alas, I am more determined to see there are future books to fill with such tributes than my lungs are determined to draw their next breath.

However, I will leave you with this: Dear Reader, my final thanks are saved for you- for having that faith in me we talked about in the beginning of this book. I hope you found it well-placed. I hope you found this journey to be one worth taking.

And if it wasn't? Well, like I said . . .

It's probably too late.

In fact, I'd say you're looking a tad bit feverish already.

Miles Mendoza is a New York City based writer. He has been making bad decisions since day one and has learned absolutely nothing from any of them. One time, after a not so quick stint in the Marine Corps, this fucker conned Columbia University into granting him admission to their undergraduate program. Prior to beginning his classes there, he made the fatal mistake of learning that Hunter S. Thompson had also once schmoozed his way onto the campus after leaving the Air Force, before mysteriously disappearing from their rosters without a hint as to the reason why. With that dangerous nugget of dynamite burrowed deep into his subconscious, it's no surprise this wannabe-intellectual turned good-for-nothing thrill-seeker eventually ditched his Ivy League classes to attach himself to the teat of the city's working-class underbelly as an EMT. He's been working emergency services in some form or another ever since. Eventually, this degenerate met a wonderful nurse, Petra, who appeared to have great prospects in this world. Naturally, he did the worst thing he could think to do to the poor woman and married her. She and their cute dog, Bruce, are now cursed to live out their lives with this asshole while he demands they read endless revisions of poems and short stories he scribbled out during work breaks. When not writing, this total pest can be found rambling on to friends about how he's traded in a drinking habit for running- just before pressuring them to describe, in great detail, the flavor profile of the whiskey they're currently sipping. This man is an absolute public nuisance and should be avoided at all costs. If you see him, immediately leave the area and consider sending a tip to your local FBI office... just in case.

Made in the USA
Las Vegas, NV
05 February 2022